EXTREME SPORTS BIOGRAPHIES™

TAÏG KHRIS
In-Line Skating Champion

Ian F. Mahaney

The Rosen Publishing Group's
PowerKids Press™
New York

To my favorite niece, Claire

Safety gear, including helmets, wrist guards, kneepads, and elbow pads, should be worn while in-line skating. Do not attempt tricks without proper gear, instruction, and supervision.

Published in 2005 by The Rosen Publishing Group, Inc.
29 East 21st Street, New York, NY 10010

First Edition

Editor: Heidi Leigh Johansen
Book Design: Mike Donnellan
Photo Researcher: Peter Tomlinson

Cover, pp. 4 (bottom), 12, 15, 22 © Nicolas Sautiez / ACM / CORBIS; pp. 4 (top left), p. 19 (right) © Tony Donaldson / Icon SMI / Rosen Publishing; p. 4 (top right) © AbleStock / Index Stock Imagery; p. 7 (top) © Icon SMI; p. 7 (bottom) © MAPS.com / CORBIS; p. 8 © Duomo / CORBIS; pp. 8 (inset), 11, 16 Tony Donaldson / Icon SMI; p. 16 (inset) UPI Photo Service; p. 19 (left) Zack Podell / Icon SMI; p. 20 (left) © Al Fuchs / NewSport / CORBIS; p. 20 (right) © Larry Kasperek / NewSport / CORBIS.

Library of Congress Cataloging-in-Publication Data

Mahaney, Ian F.
  Taïg Khris : in-line skating champion / Ian F. Mahaney.— 1st ed.
    v. cm. — (Extreme sports biographies)
  Includes bibliographical references and index.
  Contents: Extreme in-line skating — Getting to know Taïg Khris — Taïg Khris, aggressive in-line skater — Taïg gets competitive — Rookie of the year — A winner — Taïg's double backflip — Extreme safety — The double flatspin — Taïg's other lives.
  ISBN 1-4042-2746-6 (lib. bdg.)
  1. Khris, Taïg, 1975—Juvenile literature. 2. Roller skaters—Algeria—Biography—Juvenile literature. 3. In-line skating—Juvenile literature. [1. Khris, Taïg, 1975– 2. Roller skaters. 3. In-line skating. 4. Extreme sports.] I. Title. II. Series.

  GV858.22.K47M35 2005
  796.21—dc22

                        2003023264

Manufactured in the United States of America

Contents

Taïg Khris is a famous in-line skating star. He learned how to roller-skate on quad skates, above right, which are boots that have two wheels in the front and two in the back. Taïg started using in-line skates, above left, when he was 21.

Extreme In-Line Skating

Extreme in-line skating, also called **aggressive** skating, is a type of roller-skating in which skaters wear in-line skates and **perform** hard tricks. The term "in-line skating" may sound strange at first, but it really makes sense. An in-line skate has a single row of wheels that are in a line, like the blade of an ice skate.

The first type of popular roller-skating was quad skating. Quad skating is probably what you think of when you imagine **traditional** roller skates. Quad skating has been popular for about 140 years. In 1980, two brothers from Minnesota started a company that made roller skates with in-line wheels. Soon in-line skates became faster and safer, and they provided better exercise than quad skates did. Taïg Khris is a world-famous in-line skating **champion** who performs some of the most daring in-line skating moves today.

Taïg Khris was born on July 27, 1975, in Algeria. Algeria is a country in northern Africa that borders the Mediterranean Sea. Taïg's mother is of Greek **descent** and his father is of Algerian descent. Taïg's name sounds like "TAH-eeg." Taïg and his family moved to France when Taïg was a young boy. Taïg is a citizen of both France and Greece. At six years old, Taïg tried roller-skating for the first time. Soon Taïg began doing simple tricks. He quickly fell in love with skating. Taïg and his brother skated in Paris, France, where Taïg's family lived. When Taïg tried in-line skates at age 21, he found it easier to ride the **half-pipe**. Taïg became skilled on in-line skates quickly because he practiced hard. He watched skating videos and tried new tricks. Taïg was on his way to becoming one of the best in-line skaters in the world!

Taïg rides a top-of-the-line half-pipe. There are many ways people can use in-line skates. In-line skaters exercise, perform tricks, play hockey, race, and zigzag through cones. Inset: Taïg was born in Algeria, which is in northern Africa.

Roller skaters have often skated and performed tricks in empty swimming pools. Skaters also use half-pipes, such as this one. It takes a lot of practice to master half-pipe moves! Inset: Taïg flies high over a Santa Monica, California half-pipe. He first tried riding a half-pipe on quad skates as a teenager.

Taïg Khris, Aggressive Skater

Taïg Khris is an aggressive skater. Aggressive skating is an **extreme sport**. Taïg's specialty is performing tricks on a half-pipe. A half-pipe is a U-shaped skating **ramp**. Skateboarders and in-line skaters love to use the half-pipe to perform tricks. Taïg first tried skating on a half-pipe when he was 15 years old, on quad skates. Now Taïg uses in-line skates and can go even faster. Taïg begins by standing on one side of the half-pipe. He skates down into the half-pipe and his **momentum** carries him to the other side, where he jumps into the air and performs a trick, such as a flip in midair. Then Taïg lands and skates down the half-pipe and his momentum takes him up the other side to perform another trick. In in-line skating **competitions,** the half-pipe event is called vert, which stands for "**vertical**." Another event, called the park event, is a course with different jumps, railings, and ramps.

Taïg Gets Competitive

The Aggressive Skaters Association (ASA) is a company that plans aggressive skating competitions worldwide. Every summer, the ASA holds a **professional**, or pro, tour and an **amateur** tour. A tour is a competition of several aggressive skating events that are held in different places throughout the summer and the fall. The places to which the tour goes are called tour stops. In the summer of 1996, Taïg turned 21 years old while skating with the ASA Amateur Tour. Anyone can skate with the ASA Amateur Tour because it is for people at any skill level who do a sport for fun. That year, thousands of people, including Taïg, skated with the ASA Amateur Tour. The skaters had fun and cheered on fellow skaters. One of Taïg's first competitions on the tour was in Paris, France. Taïg, a new competitor in the in-line skating world, did very well. He finished in fifth place in that competition.

Taïg performs a trick using the edge of the half-pipe in a 1997 ASA event in Philadelphia, Pennsylvania. Inset: Taïg, wearing a white shirt, takes a moment to relax in the sun after a competition in California with fellow in-line skater Cesar Mora.

Taïg performs a twisting half-pipe trick. Taïg has done very well at many competitions, including the ASA Pro Tour, the X Games, and the Gravity Games.

Rookie of the Year

In 1997, Taïg Khris became a pro. That means that in-line skating became Taïg's full-time job. He competes against the best aggressive skaters in the world. Joining the ASA Pro Tour is not easy to do. Each year only about 30 riders from the ASA Amateur Tour are allowed to compete in the next year's ASA Pro Tour. For Taïg, making the ASA Pro Tour was a huge accomplishment. He had only been in-line skating for one year.

The X Games is a major stop on the professional tour. The X Games is an extreme sports competition held every year in the winter and the summer. Aggressive in-line skating, skateboarding, and wakeboarding are examples of events held at the X Games. In 1997, the X Games was held in San Diego, California. Taïg won the silver **medal** in the vert competition. Taïg did so well in his **rookie** year, or his first year as a professional, on the ASA Pro Tour that he was named Rookie of the Year.

Taïg Khris is known for skating well in competitions. Taïg does not usually get worried when he has to perform in front of a large crowd of people. Instead, he gets **excited**! This helps him to perform his bold moves so well.

The ASA Pro Tour stops at many famous events other than the X Games, including the **Gravity** Games. The Gravity Games is a competition like the X Games, featuring many extreme sports events.

In 2001, Taïg won a gold medal in the vert event at the Gravity Games in Providence, Rhode Island. He also took home his fifth X-Games medal by winning the gold in the X-Games vert event. Finishing the year by winning the 2001 ASA Pro Tour World Championships meant that Taïg was considered the best aggressive skater in the world. At 26 years old, Taïg had become a world-famous champion.

In his professional career from 1997 to 2001, Taïg competed in 103 vert events and finished with the gold medal 71 times. Taïg is daring during competitions and jumps very high into the air.

Taïg performs a bold flip. Taïg is known to be inventive with his in-line skating moves. Inset: Taïg celebrates his 2001 X-Games gold medal. He won many fans when he completed a perfect double backflip at that exciting event.

Taïg's Double Backflip

The double backflip is one of the most exciting tricks that aggressive skaters can attempt. In a double backflip, the skater rides up the half-pipe, jumps off the top, and flips backward two times before landing and then riding down the half-pipe. The top in-line skating champions, including Taïg Khris, Takeshi Yasutoko, Matt Lindenmuth, and Eito Yasutoko, can complete double backflips. However, none of these skaters will say that it is easy to do. In fact, these top riders often fall when they try to perform this **amazing** trick.

In 2001, the X Games was held in Philadelphia, Pennsylvania. That year Taïg landed two double backflips! This earned Taïg the gold medal with a score of 98.75 out of a possible 100 points. He also secured his **reputation** as a daring skater who can land the tricky double backflip most often in competition.

Extreme Safety

Aggressive skating is an exciting and active sport. Whether a skater is jumping off the half-pipe or skating to the store, it is smart to stay safe and be careful. The International Inline Skating Association (IISA) is a nonprofit group that offers safety rules for people who enjoy in-line skating. These rules are important because many tricks that in-line skaters perform can be unsafe. The rules can be shortened to four letters, S.L.A.P., which stand for Smart, **Legal**, **Alert**, and **Polite**. Even though Taïg wears safety gear, he has hurt himself many times.

Smart—Always wear safety gear, including elbow pads, kneepads, wrist guards, and a helmet.
Legal—Obey sidewalk rules and park rules.
Alert—Be on the lookout for dangers and stay in control.
Polite—Practice good manners with other skaters, bicyclists, and people who are walking.

Keep it safe when you are skating! Taïg has broken his arms, his nose, his foot, and five of his fingers. He has had surgery on his knee and his shoulder. Taïg skates with a helmet, kneepads, wrist guards, and elbow pads.

Above Left: Taïg celebrates a great score. Some people call Taïg the Magician because he practices magic as a hobby and because his skating moves look like magic! Above Right: Taïg performs a double flat spin at an outdoor park.

The Double Flat Spin

   In August 2002, the Gravity Games was held in Cleveland, Ohio. Taïg finished in fourth place that year, but he performed an amazing trick just after his official competing time was up. Taïg performed the very first double flat spin. Taïg rode the half-pipe until he reached a blazing speed on his skates. He jumped and flipped himself over so that his belly faced the ground. Then he spun around twice in midair while keeping his body straight, so that he rolled like a log. Wow! Taïg landed the trick perfectly, but his trick did not count toward his score. Still, Taïg was the first skater to complete this unbelievable trick in competition. Taïg earned the respect of many in-line skaters and fans at the Gravity Games.

   Taïg's other tricks include the alley-oop and the switch fakie 900. He also enjoys performing a 720-degree flip, or two full flips, 6 feet (2 m) in the air off the half-pipe.

Taïg's Other Lives

Taïg Khris spends most of his time practicing and competing as a professional in-line skater, but he has many hobbies, too. Thanks to traveling throughout Europe with his family as a child, Taïg speaks five languages. He plays the **piano**, acts, and dances. In his free time, Taïg enjoys spending time with his family. Taïg is a very skilled wakeboarder, snowboarder, and tennis player. Taïg also runs a skate shop and a ramp company. At the Taïg Khris Ramp School at Club Med, Taïg teaches beginners the basics of in-line skating and shows more advanced riders how to ride the  half-pipe. Taïg is a featured skater in a video game called Aggressive Inline. Each skater in the video game performs a **unique** trick. Taïg's unique trick is the double backflip, of course!

Glossary

aggressive (uh-GREH-siv) Bold and daring.

alert (uh-LERT) Paying attention to what is going on around you.

amateur (A-muh-tur) Someone who lacks practice in something.

amazing (uh-MAYZ-ing) Excellent.

champion (CHAM-pee-un) The best, or the winner.

competitions (kom-pih-TIH-shinz) Games.

descent (dih-SENT) The line of family from which someone comes.

excited (ik-SYT-ed) Stirred up.

extreme sport (ek-STREEM SPORT) A bold and uncommon sport, such as BMX, inline skating, motocross, skateboarding, snowboarding, and wakeboarding.

gravity (GRA-vih-tee) The natural force that causes objects to move toward Earth.

half-pipe (HAF-pyp) A ramp that is shaped like a big *U*.

legal (LEE-gul) Allowed by the law.

medal (MEH-dul) A small, round piece of metal given as a prize.

momentum (moh-MEN-tum) The strength or force gained through a body's motion.

perform (per-FORM) To carry out, to do.

piano (pee-A-noh) An instrument with small hammers that strike strings to make music.

polite (puh-LYT) Behaving well in front of others.

professional (pruh-FEH-shuh-nul) Paid for what he or she does.

ramp (RAMP) A sloping platform.

reputation (reh-pyoo-TAY-shun) The ideas people have about another person.

rookie (RU-kee) Referring to a player's first year.

traditional (truh-DIH-shuh-nul) Usual.

unique (yoo-NEEK) One of a kind.

vertical (VER-tih-kul) In an up-and-down direction.

Index

Web Sites

Due to the changing nature of Internet links, PowerKids Press has developed an online list of Web sites related to the subject of this book. This site is updated regularly. Please use this link to access the list: www.powerkidslinks.com/esb/khris/